Original title:
The Feeling Dance

Copyright © 2024 Creative Arts Management OÜ
All rights reserved.

Author: Victor Mercer
ISBN HARDBACK: 978-9916-88-998-5
ISBN PAPERBACK: 978-9916-88-999-2

Embracing Every Twirl

In the dance of light, we sway,
With every step, we find our way.
The world around us fades away,
In this moment, we choose to stay.

Whirling like leaves upon the breeze,
We twirl with joy, we move with ease.
Each spin a whisper to the skies,
In laughter's echo, our spirit flies.

Hearts entwined in this vibrant space,
Lost in the rhythm, we find our grace.
Every twirl a story untold,
In gentle warmth, our dreams unfold.

Under the stars, we spin and glide,
With every twirl, our souls collide.
Embracing all, both near and far,
In love's true dance, we find who we are.

Syncopation of Souls

In the rhythm of night, we sway,
Hearts beat in a wild array,
Tangled in melodies soft,
As the stars above drift aloft.

Notes echo in whispered dreams,
Carving paths like silver streams,
In the silence, we find sound,
In the chaos, love is found.

Embrace of Fleeting Moments

Time dances like falling leaves,
Whispering secrets as it weaves,
In the blink of an eye, they fade,
Leaving traces of memories made.

Every heartbeat, a fleeting glance,
Life's brief waltz, a tender chance,
Hold tight to the warmth that glows,
In the now, where true love grows.

Spirals of Joy and Sorrow

Laughter mingles with soft sighs,
In every tear, a truth lies,
Joy and sorrow, a twisted thread,
Weaving tales of the paths we tread.

Like a dance on the edge of time,
We ascend, and we sometimes climb,
In the spiral, we find our fate,
A cycle of love that will wait.

Dance of Unspoken Words

Eyes speak volumes, silence loud,
In the space where hearts are bowed,
Each glance, a verse, a refrain,
In the quiet, love sings its pain.

Hands brush lightly, a gentle spark,
In the shadows, where dreams embark,
Let the music play on and on,
In the dance, we find our dawn.

Traces of Laughter

In the echoes of the night,
Soft giggles drift and play,
Memories wrapped in light,
Chasing shadows away.

Footprints on the golden sand,
Whispers of joy remain,
A fleeting, gentle hand,
With laughter's sweet refrain.

The world glimmers with glee,
Each chuckle holds a spark,
A melody so free,
Dancing in the dark.

In the heart, a warm embrace,
Where joy and hope collide,
Traces of a happy place,
In laughter, we abide.

Fusion of Dreams

A canvas painted bright,
With hopes and visions bold,
Woven in the soft twilight,
A tapestry of gold.

Stars collide in the night sky,
Creating worlds anew,
Whispers on the wind sigh,
As dreams begin to brew.

Through the haze of silver mist,
Desires start to soar,
In the heart, a gentle twist,
Forever seeking more.

In this fusion, we arise,
Connected, hand in hand,
With every tear, every rise,
In dreams, together stand.

Tangle of Emotions

Heartstrings pull and sway,
In a dance of hope and fear,
A tangled web we play,
Drawn ever near, ever dear.

Joy and sorrow intertwine,
A spectrum of the soul,
In every touch, a sign,
Of love that makes us whole.

Gentle whispers in the night,
Echoes of longing hearts,
In shadows, flickers of light,
As the silence imparts.

The journey we embark,
With laughter, tears in store,
In this tangle, we spark,
A bond that asks for more.

Staccato of Longing

Heartbeat quickens the night,
A rhythm soft and clear,
With every pause, a fright,
In longing, we draw near.

Moments flash like bright stars,
Scattered across the sky,
Bridges built with our scars,
Unspoken, we comply.

In the silence, we find space,
Time dances in our veins,
Every glance, a trace,
Of love's sweet hidden pains.

The staccato of our dreams,
A melody to hold,
In this longing, it seems,
Our hearts forever bold.

Kaleidoscope of Movement

Whirls of color spin and blend,
Each turn a story, each twist a friend.
Nature dances in vibrant grace,
Life's rhythms echo, embrace the space.

Patterns emerge, a joyful sight,
Captured moments in pure delight.
Fractals of joy, bursts of cheer,
A visual symphony, bright and clear.

Synchronized Souls in Flight

Two hearts beat in a perfect song,
Together they rise, where dreams belong.
Through the air, they glide as one,
A dance of love, just begun.

Wings unfurl in the golden light,
In harmony, they chase the night.
Boundless skies are theirs to roam,
In each other's eyes, they find home.

Melodies Beneath the Surface

Soft whispers flow through silent streams,
Echoes of hopes and fragile dreams.
Beneath the waves, sweet tones arise,
A hidden world, where magic lies.

Notes entwined in a gentle swell,
Stories beneath the ocean dwell.
In depths unknown, a song takes flight,
Carried on currents, out of sight.

Waltz of the Unseen

Invisible threads weave through the night,
Guiding our steps, holding us tight.
A silent dance in moonlit grace,
Time stands still in this cherished space.

Whispers of love linger like dew,
In the shadows, our spirits flew.
Each gentle touch, a promise made,
In the waltz of life, we are unafraid.

The Art of Moving Hearts

In silence, whispers softly flow,
The canvas holds what we should know.
With colors bright, emotions blend,
A masterpiece, our hearts transcend.

Through gentle strokes, connections spark,
Each heartbeat sings, ignites the dark.
In every glance, a story told,
The art of love, both brave and bold.

Tides of Emotion Unfurled

Waves crash gently on the shore,
Secrets hidden, tales galore.
The sea reflects, our inner strife,
Tides of emotion shape our life.

With each retreat, we find our ground,
Lost and found, love's echoes sound.
In every rise, a chance to heal,
The ocean's song, a soulful feel.

Graceful Instincts Awakening

In moonlit dance, our souls take flight,
Graceful instincts, pure delight.
With every twirl, we learn to trust,
In each embrace, love's sacred dust.

As petals bloom in morning light,
Awakened hearts begin their flight.
Nature's call, a gentle guide,
In graceful moves, we now abide.

Flickers of Passion Under Stars

Beneath the vast and starlit sky,
Flickers of passion make us sigh.
Each twinkle holds a whispered dream,
A love that flows, a silent stream.

In shadows deep, desires ignite,
Two souls connect in soft moonlight.
With every spark, our hearts align,
Under the stars, your hand in mine.

Pas de Deux in the Dust

In the twilight's soft embrace,
Two shadows blend and sway,
Fleeting steps of grace,
As night invites the day.

A dance upon the floor,
Of memories adorned,
Each heartbeat opens doors,
Where love is reborn.

Whirling through the haze,
Their laughter fills the air,
Caught in a timeless phase,
With whispers meant to share.

In the dust, they find light,
A spark in every turn,
As stars ignite the night,
For passion ever burns.

Journey through Emotional Landscapes

Through valleys deep and wide,
Feelings ebb and flow,
A gentle, guiding tide,
Where heartaches come and go.

Mountains rise with might,
Each peak tells a tale,
Of joys that take flight,
And sorrows that assail.

In forests lush and green,
Shadows softly play,
Hidden paths unseen,
Lead the heart astray.

As rivers carve their song,
The journey unfolds,
Each moment, right or wrong,
A story to be told.

Euphoria in Motion

In a whirl of color bright,
Joy dances through the night,
Each smile a spark of cheer,
Lifting spirits ever near.

With every step, we soar,
Hearts alight like fire,
Euphoria we explore,
United in our desire.

A symphony unfolds,
In rhythm, we collide,
A tale of love retold,
With passion as our guide.

In motion, we are free,
A whirlwind of delight,
Euphoria's melody,
A dance that feels just right.

Whispers of Rhythm

In the silence of the night,
Soft whispers start to flow,
Rhythm takes a flight,
In dreams, we come to know.

A heartbeat in the dark,
Guiding every sway,
Each pulse a tiny spark,
Leading us away.

Through the echoes of grace,
We find our hidden song,
In the stillness, we chase,
The notes that feel so strong.

With every whispered line,
The universe in tune,
Together we entwine,
As night surrenders soon.

The Pulse of Life Beyond Words

In the quiet, hearts beat strong,
Resonating like a timeless song.
Whispers linger in the air,
Life unfolds, beyond compare.

Colors dance in shadowed light,
Flickers of truth, burning bright.
Each moment a fleeting grace,
A tapestry, life we embrace.

In silence, thoughts intertwine,
A bond unspoken, yet divine.
Time flows gently, a river wide,
In its current, we all confide.

Unseen threads weave through the day,
Marking the journeys, come what may.
The pulse of life, a sacred chord,
Beyond words, we are assured.

Resonance of Silent Echoes

In the stillness, echoes ring,
Soft reminders that life can sing.
Moments captured in twilight's hue,
Faint whispers of me and you.

Beneath the stars, dreams take flight,
Painting the canvas of the night.
In quietude, our hearts align,
Resounding beats in sacred time.

The shadows hold the stories told,
In every silence, secrets unfold.
We're drawn together, near and far,
Guided by a gentle star.

Let us cherish the unspoken ties,
Where every glance, a soft reprise.
Resonance flows, like rivers in dreams,
In silent echoes, nothing's as it seems.

Cascade of Intimate Moments

Drops of joy in soft embrace,
Each a memory, a cherished trace.
Cascading laughter, sweet and light,
Moments glimmer like stars at night.

Gentle sighs in the morning air,
Wrapped in warmth, a tender care.
In the chaos, we find the calm,
A soothing touch, a gentle balm.

Every glance, a brush of fate,
We create a world, hearts elate.
Whispers of love, secrets to keep,
In this dance, our souls leap.

Together we weave the fabric tight,
Moments shared, pure delight.
In this cascade, we forever flow,
Intimate wonders, we gently sow.

Flux of Intertwined Lives

In a world where paths converge,
Fates entwined, emotions surge.
The dance of souls, a vibrant thread,
In every heartbeat, words unsaid.

Waves of laughter meet a sigh,
Underneath the vast, open sky.
In the ebb and flow, we learn to grow,
Every moment a shared glow.

Hands reaching out, in tender grace,
Every touch a warm embrace.
Fragments of time, we hold so dear,
In this flux, we conquer fear.

As seasons change, our stories blend,
Together in the chaos, we transcend.
Lives intertwined in vibrant hues,
In the flux, we dare to choose.

Unfolding Stories in Motion

Every step tells a tale,
Woven in whispers of time.
The path unfolds like a scroll,
With secrets tucked between the lines.

The sun dips low in the day,
Casting shadows on dreams.
Echoes of laughter linger,
As memories dance in beams.

Each moment a petal anew,
Breathing life to the once still.
Stories flow like rivers wide,
Carving hearts with intention and will.

In the hush of twilight's embrace,
Futures blend with the past.
Embers of hope softly glow,
While journeys always last.

Heartstrings Entwined in Rhythm

In the quiet of evening's grace,
Two souls find their song.
Notes cascade like gentle rain,
Binding what feels so strong.

With every heartbeat a promise,
The dance of life begins.
Twirling 'neath the silver moon,
Where love never thins.

Echoing laughter lights the dark,
A symphony of delight.
With fingers laced in a melody,
Creating magic from the night.

Together they sway, free and bold,
Every rhythm feels like home.
Heartstrings pull in perfect tune,
In this world where they roam.

Captivating Energy in the Air

Electric vibes all around,
A spark ignites the night.
Colors whirl in vibrant hues,
Setting hearts alight.

Each breath taken feels alive,
As dreams swirl like a kite.
Whispers carried on the breeze,
Lift the spirit's flight.

Laughter ripples through the crowd,
Unity in the roar.
Moments woven with pure joy,
Eagerly we explore.

The music pulses, thumping strong,
An anthem sung as one.
In this space of wild abandon,
The night has just begun.

Shapes of Unadulterated Bliss

In a field of sunlit dreams,
The flowers stretch and sway.
Each petal a canvas of joy,
Painting a bright new day.

Laughter dances on the breeze,
As shadows gently play.
Moments captured in the glow,
Of innocence at play.

Clouds drift lazily above,
In a sky so vast and blue.
Every breath a drop of peace,
Reflections of all that's true.

Here in this world of wonder,
Time slows its hurried pace.
Shapes of happiness take flight,
In this wild, sacred space.

Rhythms of Emotion

In shadows cast by silent dreams,
The heart beats soft with gentle streams.
Swirling thoughts, a dance in time,
Each pulse a whisper, a fleeting rhyme.

Colors blend in twilight skies,
With every breath, the spirit flies.
Echoes linger, moments hold,
A tapestry of stories told.

Joy and sorrow entwine as one,
A melody under the setting sun.
With every tear, a flower grows,
In the garden where true love flows.

So let the music play so sweet,
In life's embrace, we find our beat.
Every heartbeat, a step we take,
To learn, to love, to freely break.

Choreography of Heartbeats

Dancers weave in whispered nights,
Each heartbeat sparks the softest lights.
Steps in sync with fate's own plan,
An unspoken bond, a timeless span.

Rhythm builds like waves on shore,
Carving paths forevermore.
With every sway, we find our way,
In the ballet where shadows play.

Step by step, we reach the sky,
Finding love in every sigh.
Twirling softly, souls align,
A symphony, pure and divine.

Chasing dreams like fleeting stars,
We dance beneath the midnight bars.
Together we spin, a perfect flow,
In this dance, our hearts will glow.

Tides of Euphoria

On the shore where dreams collide,
Tides of joy pull me inside.
Waves of laughter crash anew,
As sunlight melts the morning dew.

Floating high on clouds of bliss,
Moments whisper, none to miss.
Each swaying wave, a secret told,
In depths of hope, we find our gold.

Feel the ebb, and feel the flow,
Where passions rise, and hearts will know.
In the current, we drift away,
To a world where we can play.

Casting nets for dreams untold,
Through waters deep and skies so bold.
Ride the tides, my heart will soar,
In euphoria, forevermore.

Waltz of Whispers

In twilight's hush, the whispers blend,
A waltz begins, hearts transcend.
Steps so light, we glide along,
To the rhythm of a silent song.

Moonlight dances on silver leaves,
In this embrace, our spirit breathes.
Every secret, soft and clear,
In this waltz, we draw so near.

Whispers swirl like petals fall,
In the quiet, we hear the call.
Softly spoken dreams take flight,
Guided gently by the night.

In this moment, time holds still,
With every heartbeat, we feel the thrill.
Together we twirl, the world unseen,
In the waltz of whispers, we are serene.

Canvas of Colorful Emotions

Splash of red, the heart's embrace,
Shades of blue, a longing trace,
Whispers green in nature's song,
A palette where we all belong.

Yellow beams, a sunlit day,
Violet hues, dreams in sway,
Blending tones, as spirits play,
On canvas bright, hopes on display.

Whirlwind of Intimacy

In the storm where hearts collide,
Soft sensations, time's sweet stride,
Glimmers of warmth in every glance,
A wild dance, a tender chance.

Spinning close, the world a blur,
Every heartbeat, soft and sure,
Entwined souls in quiet night,
In this whirlwind, pure delight.

Unison of Hopes

Together we rise, hand in hand,
Dreams unite, a hopeful band,
Voices merge in a sacred song,
In this harmony, we belong.

A brighter dawn, with eyes set high,
We chase the stars, with wings to fly,
Each whisper fuels the fire inside,
In unison, we shall not hide.

Threads of Passion

Woven tight with yearning threads,
Colors bold in the life we've led,
Passions burn like a fierce flame,
In each stitch, love's sweet name.

Textures soft, and edges raw,
Crafting dreams from the passion's core,
Every knot tells a tale so deep,
In these threads, our secrets keep.

Tangles of Emotion and Grace

In shadows deep where whispers dwell,
Hearts twist and turn, a fragile shell.
Echoes dance in silent night,
Lost in thoughts, we seek the light.

Threads of joy and threads of pain,
Woven tightly, yet we gain.
Moments fleeting, passions bloom,
Within the chaos, find your room.

Graceful steps on troubled ground,
In the silence, solace found.
Emotions swirl like autumn leaves,
In tangled paths, the heart believes.

Softly spoken, tender eyes,
In hidden truths, the courage lies.
Through the tangle, beauty grows,
In the heart, a garden glows.

Celebration of the Unheard

In corners dim where voices fade,
A symphony of souls displayed.
The silent songs begin to rise,
In whispered dreams, the spirit flies.

Lost in shadows, yet we shine,
In unspoken words, we entwine.
With every breath, a tale unfolds,
In quiet hearts, a fire holds.

Underneath the surface lies,
A world of hope, where courage flies.
Celebrating all that's untold,
In every heart, a truth to hold.

Together bound in unseen threads,
In the silence, a legacy spreads.
Through every silence, we find our song,
A celebration, where we belong.

Symphony of the Senses

Awakened morn, the sunlight plays,
In colors bright, throughout the days.
The scent of rain upon the ground,
In every heartbeat, joy is found.

Soft whispers brush against the skin,
The taste of love, where dreams begin.
A melody in rustling leaves,
In nature's arms, the spirit breathes.

The dance of shadows, bright and bold,
In every moment, stories told.
Through every sense, we intertwine,
A symphony that feels divine.

In harmony, our souls connect,
Emotion's canvas, life perfect.
Let every moment be the song,
In the symphony, we all belong.

Whirlwind of Emotion

Caught in a storm of thoughts and dreams,
Life's a dance, or so it seems.
Emotions clash like thunder's roar,
In the whirlwind, we seek the shore.

Tears like rain, feelings collide,
Through the tempest, we confide.
Each twist and turn begins to tell,
A story crafted from passion's swell.

In the chaos, we find our way,
Anchored hearts that dare to stay.
Holding on through wildest rides,
In the tempest, love abides.

Whirlwinds fade, but echoes last,
In the aftermath, shadows cast.
Together strong, though storms may roam,
In the whirlwind, we find our home.

Flow of Time and Emotion

Time trickles softly, a river flows,
Emotions dance lightly, like petals do.
Memories linger, like shadows cast,
In the quiet moments, we find our past.

Each heartbeat echoes, a whispered tune,
Love intertwines, beneath the moon.
Seasons change, but feelings remain,
In the gentle rhythm, joy and pain.

Whirls of Spontaneous Delight

Laughter bursts forth, like bursts of spring,
Moments of joy, in spontaneity they sing.
Chasing the sun, we run free and wild,
Life is a canvas, where we are the child.

Colors collide, in a vibrant spree,
Each day an adventure, what will it be?
We dance in the shadows, we twirl in the light,
Pure and unguarded, hearts take flight.

Movements of our Inner Light

In the stillness of night, we find our way,
Guided by the glow, of dreams that sway.
Wonders awaken, as thoughts take flight,
Within our souls, a gentle light.

We move with grace, in the darkest hours,
Finding our strength, in the blooming flowers.
With courage ignited, we step ahead,
Chasing the whispers, of what lies unsaid.

Journey Beyond the Horizon

Horizons beckon where the sky meets the sea,
Adventure awaits, just waiting for me.
With each step forward, I leave behind fears,
In the vast unknown, my spirit clears.

Mountains may rise, and valleys may fall,
But I'm driven by something, a passion's call.
Through storms and sunshine, I'll carve my way,
On this journey of life, come what may.

Harmony Within Chaos

In the storm we find our peace,
Whispers of calm, a gentle lease.
Chaos dances, yet we breathe,
In fervent rhythm, hearts believe.

Amid the noise, a tranquil song,
Voices blend, where all belong.
Finding light in darkest night,
Harmony's grace, a guiding light.

Fractured paths weave stories bold,
In chaos, secrets still unfold.
Let the wild winds guide our fate,
For in disorder, we create.

With each heartbeat, we embrace,
This vibrant, ever-changing space.
The world may spin, yet we remain,
In harmony, we feel no pain.

Expressions that Soar

Words like birds take flight and roam,
Painting skies, they dare to comb.
Each phrase a brush, each thought a hue,
In petals soft, emotions grew.

Dreams unfurl on wings of grace,
In every heart, a sacred place.
Voices rise, like music's tide,
With every note, our truths collide.

Stories whispered, secrets shared,
In fleeting moments, love declared.
Through laughter's echo, pain's retreat,
Expressions bloom, a world complete.

Let the silence speak aloud,
Amid the chatter, stand so proud.
In verse and rhyme, our spirits soar,
Together, we unlock the door.

Choreography of the Soul

Step by step, the soul will sway,
In a dance, we find our way.
Each movement tells a tale untold,
In the rhythm, life unfolds.

Turning tides and shifting sands,
The universe, in gentle hands.
We twirl beneath the stars so bright,
Choreographing our delight.

In each heartbeat, a pulse divine,
The sacred art, a grand design.
With every leap, we break the mold,
In this ballet, we are bold.

Let the music guide our fate,
In this moment, we create.
The spirit sings, the body flows,
In the dance, our essence glows.

Merging Melodies of Life

In every note, a story blends,
Melodies where journey bends.
Life's symphony, a sweet embrace,
In gentle chords, we find our place.

Harmony in dissonance found,
Each heartbeat makes a sacred sound.
Voices intertwine, weaves a thread,
In this tapestry, we are led.

Echoing through both joy and strife,
Music shapes the tale of life.
In moments quiet, songs arise,
Turning whispers into skies.

Together we'll compose the theme,
In every glance, a shared dream.
Merging melodies, hearts in flight,
In unity, we find the light.

Crescendo of Unspoken Words

In silence, whispers start to swell,
A tale untold, a secret spell.
Echoes linger in the air,
Unheard confessions, a heavy flare.

Beneath the surface, feelings grow,
Yearning hearts, a quiet glow.
Voids of sound, yet hearts align,
In every pause, your hand in mine.

The tension builds, a sweet refrain,
A symphony of joy and pain.
In every glance, the truth ignites,
A world created in moonlit nights.

Together, we'll find that sacred place,
Where silence blooms, and words embrace.
In every breath, a song we weave,
A crescendo born of hearts that believe.

Interlude of Togetherness

In harmony, we find our core,
A gentle bond that begs for more.
Laughter dances on the breeze,
Time stands still, our hearts at ease.

Side by side, we share our dreams,
A tapestry of love's bright beams.
The world outside may fade away,
But in this moment, we will stay.

Through trials faced and joy fulfilled,
In unity, our hearts are thrilled.
With every step, our spirits soar,
Together, we are so much more.

An interlude, a sweet embrace,
In every glance, a warm trace.
A timeless dance, a cherished song,
Together, we endlessly belong.

Dance of Colors in the Mind

Brushstrokes vivid, thoughts set free,
A palette bright, a symphony.
In twilight hues, our visions twirl,
Dreams unfurl in a vibrant swirl.

Each shade a whisper, every tone,
A canvas where our spirits roam.
With every thought, the colors blend,
A masterpiece that has no end.

In quiet moments, shades arise,
A dance of hues beneath the skies.
In the spectrum, we come alive,
In creative ecstasy, we thrive.

Let's paint the world with laughter's spark,
Each stroke a light, igniting dark.
In every color, feelings gleam,
A dance of colors, a vivid dream.

Rhythmic Journeys of the Spirit

In silent beats, the heart will roam,
Across the vast, we find our home.
Waves of time and space collide,
In rhythmic journeys, we'll abide.

Each step a pulse, a sacred tie,
In every heartbeat, we will fly.
Through mountains high and valleys low,
Our spirits glide, in ebb and flow.

With every breath, a rhythm's call,
The dance of life, we surrender all.
In harmony with time and grace,
We find our strength in every place.

Together we'll walk this endless road,
In every moment, share the load.
In rhythmic journeys, truth unfolds,
A song of souls in stories told.

Spirit of Freedom in Motion

In fields where wild winds play,
Dancers leap, hearts in sway.
The rhythm calls, the spirit flies,
Underneath the open skies.

Whispers of the morning light,
Guiding souls, a shared flight.
Hands entwined, we break the chain,
In unity, we shed the pain.

With every turn, we find our way,
Through shadows that once led astray.
The pulse of freedom in our veins,
Together, we will stake our claims.

Embrace the journey, feel the beat,
As one, we revel in our feet.
The Spirit soars where dreams ignite,
In motion, we create our light.

Unison of Hearts and Feet

Two bodies moving side by side,
In harmony, we take our stride.
A dance that breathes, a love anew,
Together, nothing we can't do.

In crowded rooms or open space,
Each step, a joy we can't replace.
The rhythm flows, our spirits blend,
In this moment, we transcend.

Eyes that meet with sacred ease,
In silent whispers, hearts appease.
A tapestry of souls at play,
Unison guides us on our way.

Through laughter bright and shadows near,
We dance away the weight, the fear.
With every beat, our spirits rise,
United hearts beneath the skies.

Dance of Fathomless Dreams

Beneath the stars, we chase the night,
In swirling tales of pure delight.
Each movement speaks of hopes untold,
In dreams where souls and truths unfold.

The air is thick with whispered schemes,
In every spin, we dance our dreams.
A silent pact, a yearning gaze,
In fathomless depths, the spirit sways.

Through moonlit paths, our shadows play,
In vibrant hues, we find our way.
The dance ignites a fire within,
In fathomless spaces, we begin.

With every leap, we touch the skies,
Beyond the limits, our heart complies.
In the dance of dreams, we truly see,
The beauty of who we're meant to be.

Interwoven Paths of Joy

Footprints traced in golden sand,
Every step, a story planned.
With laughter shared and smiles bright,
We weave our paths in morning light.

In gardens filled with colors bold,
Tales of friendship, warmly told.
Through winding roads, we find our way,
In unity, we greet the day.

As seasons change and shadows fall,
With open hearts, we rise and call.
The joy we seek in every dance,
Interwoven, we take our chance.

In moments brief, in memories vast,
Together, we will hold steadfast.
With every step that we explore,
Our paths of joy forever soar.

Uncharted Terrain of Emotion

In valleys deep where shadows lie,
We wander forth, no map in hand.
The echoes of a long-lost sigh,
Guide us through this silent land.

Each whispered thought, a starry trace,
Points the way through tangled fears.
With every step, we find our place,
A journey marked by hidden tears.

The ocean's roar, the mountain's height,
Bring forth the depths of joy and pain.
In twilight's glow, we find the light,
Where heart and spirit break the chain.

To navigate this vast expanse,
With courage as our steadfast guide,
We'll dance upon this wild romance,
In uncharted terrain, we confide.

Celebration of the Moment

A glance, a smile, the world ignites,
Each heartbeat sings a melody.
Amidst the rush, our spirit fights,
To savor life, to truly see.

The light that bursts, the laughter shared,
Moments woven, pure and bright.
In every breath, we are declared,
Alive and joyous, hearts in flight.

With every sunset, dreams take form,
The beauty in the present rare.
We savor warmth, embrace the storm,
In celebration, love's declare.

So let us rise with open arms,
To greet the day with cheer and grace.
In fleeting time, we find our charms,
A celebration of this space.

Cadence of Hearts Aligned

In silence shared, our souls compose,
A rhythm rich, a quiet song.
With every glance, the feeling grows,
In sync, we sway, where we belong.

The pulse of life, a tender beat,
Unfolds the warmth of love's embrace.
In harmony, two hearts repeat,
The cadence of a timeless grace.

Each whispered word, a gentle sound,
Lifts echoes high into the air.
Together now, we are unbound,
With every note, we deeply care.

So let us dance through night and day,
In perfect time, our spirits shine.
No distance can our love dismay,
Forever fixed, our hearts align.

Emotions that Glide

Like feathers soft, emotions soar,
Through skies of azure, wide and free.
In gentle whispers, we explore,
The depths of love, a simple key.

Each joy and sorrow glides like air,
An unseen flow, a dance divine.
With every heartbeat, we declare,
Life's fleeting moments intertwined.

The tides of feelings ebb and flow,
In tranquil pauses, silence speaks.
We ride the waves, both high and low,
Emotions glide, in dreams, it peaks.

So let us drift on currents bright,
Through oceans vast, where hearts confide.
In every glance, a spark ignites,
Emotions that forever glide.

Pirouette of Memories

Whispers of laughter, time unwinds,
Fleeting moments, in heart they bind.
Dancing softly, light as air,
Echoes of love, linger and share.

Fragments of joy in every swirl,
In the twilight, memories unfurl.
Lost in the music, hearts entwined,
A pirouette of dreams confined.

In the silence, shadows play,
Remnants of life, gently sway.
Through the corridors of the past,
Each memory cherished, forever cast.

Step by step, the story glows,
In the dance of time, love flows.
A timeless ballet, forever true,
In each pirouette, I find you.

Crescendo of Solitude

In the stillness, silence grows,
A solitary song that flows.
Whispers of longing in the night,
Shadows embrace, holding tight.

Notes of sorrow rise and fall,
Echoing softly, I hear the call.
Loneliness painted in hues of gray,
A crescendo of thoughts, lost in dismay.

Under the stars, I find my peace,
In solitude's arms, my worries cease.
Heartbeats echo in the dark,
A symphony of dreams, stark.

As the night deepens, warmth unfolds,
In my silence, truth beholds.
A melody woven, deep and wide,
In the crescendo, I confide.

Echoes in Motion

Through the forest, whispers chase,
Footsteps dance in a timeless space.
Nature's heartbeat, strong and free,
Echoes in motion, calling me.

Leaves like laughter, fluttering light,
In the breeze, they take their flight.
Every rustle, a tale to tell,
In the symphony, I find my spell.

Rivers murmur, stones reply,
Beneath the vast and endless sky.
Time flows onward, yet we stand still,
In the echoes, we feel the thrill.

Chasing shadows, tracing forms,
Life's dance transforms and warms.
In the movement, we all entwine,
Echoes of existence, divine.

Serenade of Shadows

In the twilight, shadows wane,
A serenade soft, whispers of rain.
Gentle sighs through the trees,
Carried away by the evening breeze.

Veils of darkness, secrets unfold,
Stories of love and dreams retold.
Moonlight bathes the world in grace,
In the shadows, we find our place.

Notes of silence fill the air,
In every breath, the heart laid bare.
Cascading echoes through the night,
A serenade that feels just right.

As the stars begin to gleam,
In the shadows, we find our dream.
With every heartbeat, this truth flows,
In the serenade, love grows.

Serenade of Swaying Souls

In twilight's glow, we sway and dance,
Two hearts entwined, lost in a trance.
The whispering winds, they softly play,
A serenade of night till break of day.

Underneath the stars, we find our way,
With every breath, in the moon's warm ray.
The magic lingers, a gentle tease,
Our souls united, drifting like leaves.

In harmony we blend, sweet melodies,
Waves of emotion, a warm summer breeze.
Together we dream, in shadows and light,
The serenade sings, through the velvet night.

As dawn approaches, we hold it near,
This melody soft, with no hint of fear.
In the quiet moments, love takes its toll,
Echoes of joy in our swaying souls.

Pulse of the Night

The moon awakes, casting its gaze,
On hidden paths and shadowed ways.
A heartbeat strong, the pulse is loud,
In whispered tones, we dance unbowed.

Stars twinkle bright in velvety skies,
With every glance, a spark that flies.
An electric thrill, the night ignites,
Our souls collide in shimmering lights.

Together we roam, through the midnight air,
Fingers entwined, no need for a care.
Each thumping rhythm guides our plight,
In the cool embrace of the endless night.

As shadows deepen, we push and pull,
The world around us fades, we feel so full.
In every heartbeat, a truth we recite,
Forever entwined in the pulse of the night.

Echoes of Laughter in the Air

Laughter rings out, a joyful sound,
In gentle breezes, it swirls around.
Children's giggles, a pure delight,
Echoes of laughter in the warm sunlight.

Memories linger as stories unfold,
In the open fields, in the soft, bright gold.
With every chuckle, our hearts take flight,
In the playful dance of day and night.

The warmth of friends, their voices blend,
In a chorus that carries, a joyful trend.
Each note resounds, in the cool, crisp air,
Echoes of laughter, a love we all share.

As shadows stretch long, the laughter remains,
Captured in moments, like soft autumn rains.
In the echoes, we find solace and care,
A celebration of life in the vibrant air.

Fluid Expressions of Being

In colors that flow, our spirits unwind,
Each brushstroke sings, a glimpse of the mind.
A canvas alive with feelings so bright,
Fluid expressions in the heart's delight.

Like rivers that dance, in currents so free,
We find our voice in the sound of the sea.
Each wave that crashes, each whisper it brings,
Unveils the beauty in small, simple things.

As shadows entwine with the warmth of the sun,
We learn to embrace all that we have done.
The journey of life in bold strokes and lines,
Fluid expressions of the soul that shines.

In every moment, so vivid, so clear,
We drink in the essence, banish the fear.
Let colors collide and the heart take flight,
In fluid expressions, we bask in the light.

Vibrations of the Unseen

Whispers dance in the air,
Silent echoes fill the night,
Shadows breathe with a flair,
In the dark, there's a light.

Through the mist, a soft tone,
Frequencies weave, intertwine,
Invisible paths we've flown,
In the stillness, we shine.

A heartbeat in the void,
Resonance found in a sigh,
Mysteries we've enjoyed,
In the silence, we fly.

Vibrations move the unseen,
In their rhythm, we dwell,
Unraveling all that's been,
In the depths, we compel.

Flickers of Delight

In the garden, petals sway,
Colors burst in morning glow,
Laughter chimes and holds sway,
Life's sweet dance, a bright show.

Moments caught in gentle breath,
Joy ignites like fireflies,
In shadows, we'll conquer death,
With each flicker, love flies.

Sparkling eyes, a playful glance,
In the dark, dreams take flight,
Let us revel in the chance,
To find magic in the night.

Embers of hope softly gleam,
In every heartbeat, a thrill,
We weave stories in a dream,
In delight, we are still.

Flow of the Inner Symphony

Melodies rise from deep within,
Harmonies hum in the soul,
Every note a sacred kin,
Together, we become whole.

Rhythmic pulses guide our way,
In the quiet, songs unfold,
Mind and heart in sweet ballet,
In the silence, we are bold.

Whispers of love in crescendo,
Echoes of laughter ring true,
Unified in this flow,
Together, me and you.

Each heartbeats a gentle chord,
In this symphony of grace,
Life's pure beauty we record,
In the music, we embrace.

Cascade of Tenderness

Gentle streams of soft embrace,
Flowing through the valleys green,
In a world that leaves a trace,
Love's sweet dance, a serene scene.

Whispers brush against the skin,
Caressing all that we know,
In the stillness, we begin,
In the warmth, our hearts grow.

Every glance, a tender touch,
Softly weaving through the day,
In your presence, I feel such,
Moments linger, never sway.

Underneath the starlit skies,
In this cascade, we are free,
Where every heartbeat ties,
In tenderness, you and me.

Harmony in the Chaos

In the whirlwind of noise, we find our beat,
Melodies rise where the wildflowers meet.
Through the tempest, a dance starts to sway,
In the chaos, our spirits won't fray.

Voices collide like waves on the shore,
Creating a symphony, longing for more.
In the discord, we learn to be free,
Harmony blossoms from what we can't see.

Gentle whispers beneath the loud cries,
A tapestry woven, where silence defies.
Through the clashes, our souls intertwine,
In chaotic beauty, our hearts will align.

Embracing the turmoil, we rise and we sing,
Finding the peace that the wild truly brings.
Together we flow, like rivers that race,
In the harmony found within time and space.

Steps of Sensation

Each footfall a story, a whisper of grace,
In the dance of life, we all have our place.
With each gentle rise, and dramatic fall,
We echo the rhythm, we answer the call.

Hearts beat like drums, setting pace for the night,
As shadows entwine, they flicker with light.
In soft, subtle motions, our spirits will glide,
With every small step, emotions collide.

Moments suspended, like dew on a leaf,
A fleeting connection, a joyful belief.
Step closer to feeling, where dreams intertwine,
In this dance of sensation, your heart will be mine.

Let the music surround us, as stars start to gleam,
In the hush of the evening, we live through a dream.
Every small movement, a story so grand,
Together we weave, through this delicate land.

Ballet of Beating Hearts

In the spotlight of love, our hearts take their flight,
A ballet of passion, a shimmering light.
Graceful in whispers, our secrets we share,
With every beat echoed, lost in the air.

Lifting our souls in the softest embrace,
Swept up in the motion, no fear in this space.
With twirls of affection, we dance through the night,
In the ballet of beating hearts, pure delight.

Every glance exchanged, a twinkle ignites,
As stars weave their stories in magical nights.
With every crescendo, our spirits will soar,
A ballet of dreams, forever encore.

We'll dance on the edge of forever and now,
With hearts as our stage, we take our bow.
In the rhythm of love, we perfectly play,
A ballet of beating hearts, come what may.

Unraveling in the Moonlight

Under the moon's gaze, secrets unfold,
In the night's soft embrace, our stories are told.
With whispers of silver, we dance through the shadows,
Unraveling truths, where the wild river flows.

Stars sprinkle the sky like dreams yet to find,
As hearts intertwine, leaving the past behind.
In the depth of the night, we shed our facade,
Under moonlit whispers, nothing feels odd.

Emotions like tides, they rise and they fall,
Echoes of laughter are heard through it all.
Lost in the stillness, where time seems to pause,
Unraveling in moonlight, we find our own cause.

So let us embrace, this miraculous night,
As the world fades away, under silver light.
In the glow of the moon, we find our true art,
Unraveling together, ever closer at heart.

A Tapestry of Touch and Sound

In whispers soft as morning dew,
Fingers glide where dreams come true.
The melody of hearts aligns,
In senses where the light entwines.

Each heartbeat echoes through the air,
A dance of souls, beyond compare.
With every note, the world transforms,
In harmonies where love conforms.

Textures woven, rich and deep,
Weaving moments we will keep.
In a tapestry of touch we find,
The sacred bond of heart and mind.

Steps on the Path of Connection

Each step a word in silent speech,
A journey where our hearts can reach.
Footprints left in gentle grace,
Lead us to a sacred place.

In glances shared, no need for sound,
As two souls merge, we are unbound.
Through twists and turns, our bond will grow,
In every moment, love will show.

With every laugh, with every sigh,
We craft a story, you and I.
Together on this path we walk,
In whispered dreams, we softly talk.

Navigating Waves of Emotion

The tide of feelings ebbs and flows,
In depths where hidden longing grows.
We ride the waves with tender care,
In surges, we find love laid bare.

Each crest of joy, each trough of pain,
Together we weather the stormy rain.
In the ocean's vast, we dive so deep,
Through whirlpools of secrets we dare to leap.

With every splash, we find our way,
In currents strong, our hearts will sway.
Each ripple echoes what we feel,
In this embrace, our souls are real.

Enchantment in Every Turn

In every curve, a spark ignites,
As pathways weave through days and nights.
With every twist, a story told,
In every moment, love unfolds.

The magic swirls in shadows cast,
In fleeting glances, futures vast.
With open hearts and eager hands,
We chart the course where wonder stands.

With whispers soft, we navigate,
Through enchanted realms, we celebrate.
In every turn, a chance to see,
The beauty found in you and me.

Rhythm of Revelations

In whispers soft, secrets unfold,
The dance of truth, bright and bold.
Each heartbeat echoes through the night,
Awakening dreams in fading light.

Shadows waltz with a flickering flame,
Illuminating paths, calling our name.
A rhythm rises, we sway in tune,
Under the gaze of a watchful moon.

In every note, a story to share,
The world's pulse quickens, we breathe the air.
Connection flows like a river wide,
In the rhythm of life, we all abide.

Join the chorus, let spirits ignite,
Together we weave, embracing the night.
As revelations dance, take hold of your fate,
In this beautiful moment, we celebrate.

Ascension of Souls through Motion

Through valleys deep, we lift our gaze,
Beyond the clouds, in cosmic ways.
With every step, our spirits soar,
In the heart of motion, we find the core.

Time drifts softly, like a feather's flight,
Guiding each soul towards the light.
Together we rise, hand in hand,
In this ascent, we take a stand.

From earth to sky, the journey unfolds,
In whispers of love, the truth is told.
Let the winds carry our dreams so high,
As we dance in the vastness of the sky.

In the unity of all who strive,
Through motion and spirit, we come alive.
Ascending together, a radiant whole,
The celestial dance of every soul.

Vibes that Bind Us

In laughter shared, we find our thread,
A tapestry woven, where all is said.
The warm embrace of hearts aligned,
In the vibes that bind, true love's defined.

Through trials faced, we stand as one,
In the gentle glow of the setting sun.
Echoes of hope in every sigh,
In this harmony, we learn to fly.

Each smile a beacon, guiding our way,
Together we navigate, come what may.
In the essence of joy, we find our role,
In the rhythm of life, we touch the soul.

With every heartbeat, a promise made,
In the vibes that bind, never to fade.
Together we journey, never apart,
In the dance of existence, we share one heart.

Fluidity of Spirits Together

Like rivers flowing, we shift and bend,
In the tide of life, we find our blend.
Each spirit dances, a fluid grace,
Embracing the journey, we find our place.

Through storms and sunshine, we ride the wave,
In the ebb and flow, it's love we save.
Connected by threads of laughter and tears,
In the bond of spirits, we conquer fears.

The art of change, we learn and grow,
In the fluidity, our true selves show.
Together we navigate the unknown,
In this sacred circle, never alone.

As rivers converge, our energies blend,
In the fluid dance, there's no end.
With every heartbeat, a silent tether,
In this unity, spirits together.

Heartbeats and Harmony

In the stillness of the night,
Rhythms dance, pure delight.
Soft whispers in the air,
Heartbeats call, we are aware.

Melodies intertwine and blend,
A symphony that has no end.
In the chaos, find the rhyme,
A timeless song woven in time.

Underneath the starry skies,
Love's embrace never lies.
Every echo tells a tale,
Of heartbeats that will never pale.

In a world that's wide and free,
Harmony's sweet decree.
Together, let our spirits soar,
In the music, always more.

Embrace of Electric Beats

Feel the surge beneath the skin,
Electricity, where dreams begin.
Light and sound collide as one,
Underneath the blazing sun.

Bass lines thump, a driving force,
Guiding us along the course.
Dancing close, hearts in sync,
In this moment, we won't blink.

Neon lights as stars above,
Pulse and energy, like love.
Echoes reverberate and soar,
In this embrace, we crave for more.

Let the rhythm take control,
As it flows into our soul.
Lost in beats, we come alive,
In this groove, we will thrive.

Chasing Shadows in the Light

In the glow of waning day,
Shadows stretch and softly sway.
Flickers dance on silver streams,
Chasing truths that haunt our dreams.

Golden hues kiss the ground,
In the silence, magic found.
Steps are light, hearts take flight,
Embracing whispers of the night.

Through the twilight, secrets creep,
In the stillness, memories seep.
Footprints left on paths so bright,
Chasing shadows, guarding light.

With each sigh, the stars ignite,
Guiding us with soft delight.
In the harmony of the dark,
We find solace, we leave a mark.

Unwritten Steps of Joy

In the morning's tender hue,
New adventures, born anew.
Every moment like a song,
In our hearts, where we belong.

Footprints on a sandy shore,
Each one beckons, calls for more.
In this journey, side by side,
With love as our trusted guide.

Laughter dances in the breeze,
Joyful echoes, hearts at ease.
Together, we shall pave the way,
Unwritten steps in bright array.

Underneath the open skies,
Endless dreams and melodies rise.
In the quiet, hear the call,
Unwritten steps, we'll take them all.

Bonds that Twirl in Time

In the shadows we dance, entwined,
Hearts echo softly, a rhythm aligned.
Moments unfold, both tender and bright,
Weaving our futures, a tapestry of light.

Laughter unfurls, a sweet serenade,
Every glance shared, a promise made.
Through the storms, we weather, we glide,
In the arms of each other, forever we bide.

Time may pass, yet we stand still,
In the harmony found, we know our will.
Like whispers of dreams, our spirits embrace,
In a world of chaos, we find our place.

Together we soar, on wings of trust,
In bonds that twirl, it is love that we must.
For within every moment, in rhythm and rhyme,
We treasure the magic, in bonds that twirl in time.

Nuances of Unvoiced Desires

Caught in a silence, we both understand,
The touch of your hand, a soft reprimand.
Words left unspoken, yet oh so clear,
In the gentle stillness, I feel you near.

Eyes like secrets, hold stories untold,
In the flicker of flame, emotions unfold.
Holding your gaze, each heartbeat ignites,
The nuances linger, like stars in the nights.

Waves of yearning, we drown and collide,
In the dance of frustration, no need to hide.
For passion's a whisper, so fragile, yet bold,
In the tapestry woven, our feelings unfold.

While the world watches, we bask in the glow,
For in quiet moments, true love we bestow.
In the mix of desire, all timidity flies,
In the echoes of silence, our hearts realize.

Spirals of Expression

Words cascade in vivid hues,
Like paint on canvas, emotions fuse.
Thoughts entwined in vibrant designs,
Every stroke tells tales that shine.

In the dance of letters, we twirl and sway,
Spirals of expression, come what may.
Each note a heartbeat, a pulse of the day,
In the symphony of joy, we lose our gray.

Artistry flows, like rivers run wide,
In moments we share, we cannot divide.
Thoughts intertwined, a labyrinth of dreams,
In the spirals of life, nothing's as it seems.

Breathe in the colors, let your heart soar,
In the melody of whispers, and long to explore.
For in every drumming, we find our release,
In spirals of expression, our spirits find peace.

Chaotic Beauty in Stillness

In the roar of the storm, find the eye,
Where chaos whispers, and stillness can lie.
Beauty unfolds in the moments we pause,
An intricate dance without any cause.

Time suspends in the throes of the fight,
In chaos we discover that stillness is light.
Each breath we take, a testament true,
To the beauty found in the chaos we brew.

Waves crash and pull, a tempest's embrace,
Yet in that wildness, we find our place.
For in every ripple, a lesson we glean,
In the mix of the tumult, peace can be seen.

Hold tight to the noise, let the dance begin,
For in chaotic beauty, life's where we win.
In stillness we gather, we learn how to cope,
In the vessel of chaos, we find our hope.

Milton Keynes UK
Ingram Content Group UK Ltd.
UKHW022007131124
451149UK00013B/1054